# Guidelines for logging, describing, and sampling cores and cuttings of coal and associated rocks at the drill site: USGS Open-File Report 79-1522

Robert G. Hobbs

The BiblioGov Project is an effort to expand awareness of the public documents and records of the U.S. Government via print publications. In broadening the public understanding of government and its work, an enlightened democracy can grow and prosper. Ranging from historic Congressional Bills to the most recent Budget of the United States Government, the BiblioGov Project spans a wealth of government information. These works are now made available through an environmentally friendly, print-on-demand basis, using only what is necessary to meet the required demands of an interested public. We invite you to learn of the records of the U.S. Government, heightening the knowledge and debate that can lead from such publications.

Included are the following Collections:

Budget of The United States Government
Presidential Documents
United States Code
Education Reports from ERIC
GAO Reports
History of Bills
House Rules and Manual
Public and Private Laws

Code of Federal Regulations
Congressional Documents
Economic Indicators
Federal Register
Government Manuals
House Journal
Privacy act Issuances
Statutes at Large

UNITED STATES DEPARTMENT OF THE INTERIOR

GEOLOGICAL SURVEY

Guidelines for logging, describing and sampling
cores and cuttings of coal and associated rocks at the drill site

By

Robert G. Hobbs

Open-File Report 79-1522
1979

Table of contents

Guidelines for logging, describing, and sampling

cores and cuttings of coal and associated rocks at the drill site

Introduction

The guidelines in this report are presented to assist in logging of drill cuttings, handling and describing core at the drill site, and sampling of cored rock and coal for subsequent laboratory analysis. A few suggestions on drilling techniques and core retrieval are included also. Mishandling and incorrect preparation of the core can result in unreliable or erroneous analytical results, largely negating the expensive drilling effort.

The proper logging of drill cuttings or cores requires experience and good judgment of the well-site geologist. All means available should be used as logging aids, including the maintenance of a harmonious and efficient working relationship with the driller. The driller's skill, knowledge, experience, and judgment can be an immeasurable aid to the geologist.

# Logging of drill cuttings

## General

A log of drill cuttings may be made by the driller (driller's log) or made from samples of cuttings by the geologist (sample logs). The cuttings are caught and described as drilling progresses or at specified intervals (for example, at 5 feet or 10 feet). The cuttings also may be bagged and then logged at a later itme by a geologist, ideally with the aid of geophysical logs that are run on completion of drilling.

Where a detailed description of the stratigraphy and lithology is required as drilling proceeds, the well-site geologist should catch samples continuously and describe the lithology and depth interval of each rock unit as it is penetrated. This type of logging is especially necessary if the objective is to identify a distinctive "marker" bed, other rock unit, or "core point" (the depth at which coring should begin). The penetration rate (feet drilled per minute) or drilling time should also be carefully observed and recorded. This information will aid in determining lithologic changes and boundaries between rock types.

# Drilling with air

Logging drill cuttings when drilling with air is easier and more accurate than when drilling with a fluid. Lithologic changes can be noted almost as soon as new rock units are penetrated, because the time it takes the rock chips to reach the surface after being cut (sample lag-time) is very short. The lag-time may be reasonably determined by closely monitoring the drill-penetration rate (in feet per minute). A distinctive "drilling break" (a quick increase or decrease in the drill-penetration rate) should be noted immediately to the nearest second. Then the drill cuttings should be logged continuously for a lithologic change. The difference between the time of the "drilling break" and the time the lithologic change was displayed by the samples is the sample lag-time; it usually is measured in seconds. This method is applicable only if the drilling break actually was caused by an observable lithologic change, rather than by some mechanical change in the drilling equipment or procedure.

The sample lag-time is a function of the velocity of the return air from the bit to the surface. The sample velocity of lag-time will generally average about one-half of the velocity depending on factors such as the depth, return water inflow, the hole diameter, and ash-outs, The optimum return air velocity generally ranges from 5,000 to 7,000 fpm (feet per minute). Air moving at velocities of less than 5,000 fpm might not be able to carry the larger cuttings out of the hole and effectively clean the hole of cuttings. The high air velocities can and usually does cause excessive hole enlargement (caverns) and subsequent caving especially in zones of incompetent or soft rock and/or coal. This differential hole enlargement causes areas of severe turbulent air flow, greatly reducing drilling effeciency and core recovery, while greatly increasing the chances of the drill pipe becoming stuck.

Return air velocity may be estimated by the following:

$$CFM = \frac{V \; (D_1{}^2) - (D_2{}^2)}{183.3} \qquad \text{Solve for V,} \qquad V = \frac{CFM \; (183.3)}{(D_1{}^2) - (D_2{}^2)}$$

CFM = cubic feet of air per minute

V = velocity of air-feet per minute

$D_1$ = diameter of hole

$D_2$ = diameter of drill rod (outside)

This formula is actually for noncompressible fluid flow, but can be used in this type application for relatively shallow holes (less than 500 ft).

An ordinary kitchen strainer, 2 in. to 8 in. in diameter (see metric-English equivalents page for conversion factors), may be used to catch the rock samples for examination. Where the cutting fragments are small and escape through the screen, such as cuttings from a friable or fine-grained sandstone or coal, a cheese-cloth filter placed on the screen is useful. Also, a flat metal deflector can be hand-held in the return airstream; it will cause the samples to fall out and assist retrieval.

The cuttings from air drilling are usually dominantly from the rock unit being drilled; contamination from the previously drilled overlying rock is minimal. Entry of the drill into a water-bearing zone is most holes, easily and accurately determined.

4

## Drilling with a fluid

When drilling with fluid (water or mud), the logging of drill cuttings requires more frequent sample catching and a more careful examination of the cuttings than when drilling with air. The cuttings usually are more contaminated by rock fragments from the upper part of the drill hole. Close observation of drilling time per foot is very important in determining lithologic changes and sample lag-time. Generally, the lag-time will become appreciable at depths of 200 feet or more for non-core drilling. If the drill penetration rate is high, these depths would be decreased accordingly. A slow penetration rate would increase the depths at which the lag-time become important.

The optimum return velocities of the drilling fluid are 200 fpm for non-core drilling and 90 fpm for core drilling. The return fluid velocity may be estimated by:

$$V = \frac{GPM \ (0.3208)}{A}$$

V = velocity of fluid in feet per minute

GPM = gallons per minute (pump output)

A = area for return velocity (A - area of drilled

hole less area of drill pipe)

A return velocity either too low or too high will have the same effects as too low or high velocities when air drilling.

The sample lag-time when drilling with a fluid is affected by the same factors as with air drilling plus the viscosity of the circulating fluid.

The samples from a rock unit being drilled will generally contain variable amounts of fragments of the overlying rock units previously drilled, depending on the competency of the overlying rocks. However, the predominant rock type in the sample is usually the rock being drilled. A concentration of fragments from a rock unit that tends to cave or wash out can be the cause of logging error. Judgment of the well-site geologist is required to recognize these extraneous fragments, and to determine the depth and lithology of the unit being drilled.

Sample logging of coal can be difficult and requires special care. The penetration of the top of a coal bed will, in most cases, result in a sudden increase in penetration rate. The base of the coal is usually marked by a decrease in the penetration rate. After drilling through a coal bed, much or most of the rock in the sample cuttings may consist of coal, the proportion decreasing as the vertical distance below the coal bed increases.

As drilling continues below the coal bed, contamination of the sample(s) by coal is due in part to the coal cuttings being recirculated through the system and in part to washing out of the coal bed. Coal cuttings, especially thinner beds, and all beds at depths greater than 350 to 400 feet may not be detected if the samples were not taken directly from the flowing fluid as near the hole as possible. The drilling fluid specific gravity, because of very fine cuttings held in suspension as well as various additives (bentonite) will approach the specific gravity of coal. This will cause the coal to remain in suspension, requiring a much longer setting time than rock cuttings.

Failure to accurately log the top and base of the drilled coal bed can result in gross overestimation of coal-bed thickness. Also, when drilling through a series of coal beds, extreme care must be used in logging the top and base of each bed.

## Logging, describing, and handling cores

### Preparation and equipment

The area selected for core logging and handling should be to one side of the drilling operation, so that the geologist and driller will not interfere with each other. It should also be located at a place where foot and vehicular traffic and dust will not be a problem and a source of possible core contamination.

Core trays should be used whenever possible, and cores should not be laid out on the ground, even on plastic sheeting. If the cores are to be logged at the drill site, a core examination table, easily and inexpensively constructed in the field, is strongly recommended. It should be built of two sawhorses at a convenient working height, with a working surface consisting of a 2 in. x 12 in. x 10 ft plank or a 3/4 in. x 12 in. x 8 ft sheet of plywood laid across them. The trays are placed in holders on the working surface.

The core trays, two or more, can also be constructed in the field. They should be at least 2 ft longer than the core barrel; that is, 12 ft for a 10-ft core barrel. Trays for small diameter core (less than 2 in.) can be constructed from 1 in. x 4 in. x 12 ft boards nailed together at right angles, with cross pieces added for stability. One end should be closed, the other left open so that the core barrel may be laid directly in the tray for core removal. For larger cores, lumber of appropriate size should be used. If the core is going to be split, 2-in.-thick lumber or steel trays should be used. Steel trays can be made locally by using straight, fair quality, thin- or medium-wall-thickness steel or plastic casing or pipe, cut in half lengthwise. The rough-cut edge can be ground down or covered with tape.

Standardizing the way core is removed from the barrel and put into the tray will prevent reversal of the core. The closed end of the tray should hold the end of the core that comes out of the core barrel first; wireline core is usually removed from the top of the core barrel, and conventional core is usually taken from the bottom.

Drilling water should be used in washing the core and in later bagging, because water from a different source could increase contamination of the core and give erroneous analytical results. Also, samples of all drilling fluid additives should be taken (See Swanson and Huffman, 1976); and sealed in plastic bags marked with project identification data, hole number, footage, date, and name of additives. These samples of additives are for possible future analysis should anomalous results appear in the rock or coal analyses.

## Core retrieval

Unless extra care is taken, core can be lost when the core barrel is pulled out of the hole. Sudden, jerky starts, high speeds, and sudden stops should be avoided. These can force the core out of the barrel or break it in the barrel, thus allowing the core to fall out as the barrel comes out of the hole.

To expedite drilling, the driller should have two inner core barrels. Once the full barrel is detached, it can be replaced by the empty barrel and run back into the hole; drilling can then be resumed and the core can be removed from the first barrel while drilling continues. This will reduce drilling time and down-time, and avoid haste during the extra time and care required for core removal.

When removing the core from the inner barrel (from the top for wireline core, or from the bottom for conventional core), care should be used. The core may hang-up or stick in the barrel. If so, the barrel should be struck gently with a rubber hammer or tapped with a wooden stick or the wood handle of a hand hammer (nothing larger). Never strike the inner barrel with a metal object such as a bar or hammer; this may dent the barrel, thereby compounding core-removal problems, and dents and warping may ultimately ruin the inner barrel. If the driller or someone else does strike the inner barrel, make sure it is his barrel, not yours.

If tapping does not release the core or if it is jammed in the barrel, the best method for removal is to pump the core out. Place a rag on top of the core and connect the barrel to the mud or air system. Apply pressure slowly and carefully, simultaneously tapping the barrel with the rubber hammer, and the core should slowly be eased out. Unless special care is used when applying and holding pressure, especially air pressure, the core jam may be suddenly released and the core may be projected over quite a wide area, making it difficult to reconstruct the correct stratigraphic sequence from the scattered fragments. Moreover, the sudden release of core can be dangerous to personnel. Hand pressure pumps are available and should be used if possible, in order to maintain more control over the pressure necessary to extrude the core.

The core should be laid out in the tray directly from the barrel, which should rest full length in the tray and be withdrawn slowly. This will help keep the core in sequence, especially broken sections of friable sandstone, weak shale, or weak or broken coal.

In areas where the core tends to stick or hang up the split tube core barrel should be used. This barrel consists of two lengthwise half sections, held together by a fiberglass tape. To remove the core the barrel is lain horizontal and the tape cut and the top section removed. The core is exposed undisturbed over its full length.

## Core logging

As soon as the core is in the tray, the core and tray should be removed from the drill area. If the core will not be logged or boxed immediately, it should be covered with a moist canvas, burlap, or other fabric, especially during the summer months. Do not use plastic sheets. During the winter months, protect the core from direct sunlight and from drying out.

The first step in logging the core is to arrange the core, as nearly as possible in its original sequence and to fit broken sections together. Intervals of lost core should be noted. Measure the length of core and compare the measurement with the cored interval recorded by the driller. The difference between the length of recovered core and the length of the cored interval indicates the amount of core lost. An attempt should be made to determine the intervals from which the core was lost. The drillers log can be of assistance if drilling breaks or changes in mud or air pressure have been noted. If the lost core interval(s) cannot be determined with reasonable certainty, footage represented by the loss should be assigned to the bottom or top, whichever is most consistent with the rock type being drilled and the core accordingly reconstructed.

Commonly, incompetent rock core will be lost at the bottom of the cored interval because the core catcher (part of the core barrel) may slip on the core, and not break the core at the base of the run. At times, a small core section at the top of the core sequence (usually only a few inches long), may be ground off at an angle to the axis of the core. This will be a core stub left in the hole from the previous run. The top of the barrel may contain mud or mudlike rock fragments that have settled in the bottom of the hole at the end of the previous run. They should be discarded.

When describing the core, a standardized order such as the following, is recommended:

For rock:

    rock type (sandstone, mudstone, etc.)

    color

    grain size

    bedding

    special features (carbonaceous, fossilferous)

    accessory minerals (pyrite, gypsum, etc.)

    relative moisture inherent, not surface wetness

    hardness

For coal:

    coal type (lignite, subbituminous), if known

    color (relative hue)

    banding:  dull and bright bands, or fusain, vitrain, etc.

    fracture (inherent, cleat, butt, or induced)

accessory minerals (pyrite, clay cleat fillings etc.)

relative moisture inherent, not surface

hardness

special features (clean, impure, earthy, etc.; tree trunk,

stems, leaves, resin, etc.)

contacts with roof, floor, and partings

Additional detains that the geologist may consider important

may be added

A suggested form for recording these data is shown on Figure 1.

Additional pages may be added as needed.

U.S. Geological Survey
Branch of Coal Resources

Project _____

Hole No. _____ Geologist _____

Type log. _____ Elev. _____ Total depth _____

Location _____ Sec. _____ T. _____ R. _____

Nearest town _____ County _____ State _____ Quad. _____

Drilled by: _____

Driller(s): _____

Drill: _____ Date start _____ Complete _____

Non-core intervals and size hole: _____

Cored intervals and size: _____

Remarks: _____
_____
_____
_____

| LOG | | | | CORE | | | |
|------|-----|--------|-------------|-----|------|------|------|
| From | To | Length | Description | No. | From To | Foot Rec'd | % Rec'd |
| | | | | | | | |
| | | | | | | | |
| | | | | | | | |
| | | | | | | | |
| | | | | | | | |
| | | | | | | | |
| | | | | | | | |
| | | | | | | | |
| | | | | | | | |
| | | | Figure 1 | | | | |
| | | | A type of Sample and/or Core | | | | |
| | | | description and logging form | | | | |
| | | | 14 | | | | |

Log Continuation:                              Hole No.:_____

Page_____of _____                           Project:_____

| LOG | | | | CORE | | | |
| --- | --- | --- | --- | --- | --- | --- | --- |
| From | To | Length | Description | No. | From To | Foot Rec'd | % Rec'd |
| | | | | | | | |
| | | | | | | | |
| | | | | | | | |
| | | | | | | | |
| | | | | | | | |
| | | | | | | | |
| | | | | | | | |
| | | | | | | | |
| | | | | | | | |
| | | | | | | | |
| | | | | | | | |
| | | | | | | | |
| | | | | | | | |
| | | | | | | | |
| | | | | | | | |
| | | | | | | | |
| | | | | | | | |
| | | | | | | | |
| | | | | | | | |
| | | | | | | | |
| | | | | | | | |
| | | | | | | | |
| | | | | | | | |
| | | | | | | | |
| | | | | | | | |
| | | | | | | | |
| | | | | | | | |
| | | | | | | | |
| | | | | | | | |
| | | | | | | | |
| | | | | | | | |
| | | | | | | | |
| | | | 15 | | | | |

Core should not be logged by examining only the outside surface. Accurate logging requires that the core be broken both laterally and longitudinally and fresh surfaces observed.

Coal, especially, must be broken both laterally and longitudinally to be accurately logged. Unbroken, black carbonaceous shale commonly cannot be distinguished from coal, especially if air drilled.

Breaking the core will expose minerals such as pyrite, marcasite, gypsum, and kaolinite deposited in minute fractures within the coal and other rocks. Coal hardness and the relative inherent moisture can best be determined by breaking the core.

During logging, the coal must not be allowed to become dry; it must be covered with a moist cloth as protection from the direct sun. Maintaining the coal core surface moisture will reduce the variability of determinations for a given coal on the as-received part of the proximate and ultimate analysis. It may be necessary from time to time to moisten the coal core surface with water to prevent the coal from drying, losing its inherent moisture and air slacking. Coal will not, as a general rule, absorb additional water interstitially, above its equilibrum moisture, providing the coal has not been allowed to dry and partially dessicate.

## Boxing of core

Several types of core boxes are available. The box most preferred for cores up to 3 inches in diameter is a sectionalized, water resistant heavy cardboard box, available commercially. However, core boxes can be built in the field to the geologists or driller's specifications and preferences; and such boxes, where the core is broken and placed side by side, or longer boxes, where the core is laid out in 10-foot length, depend on project requirements and the geologists' specifications and preference.

The outside of the box (not the lid) should have the project name, hole number, core-run number, and footage of core in the box, as well as the top and bottom of the core, date, and geologist.

Polyethylene sheet material (0.006-inch thickness, minimum) should be used to line the inside of the core box. After putting in the core, the plastic should be folded over it.

A standardized system for placing the core in the box should be used to avoid possible misinterpretation or reversal of core sections. Two systems generally used are:

1. Book fashion: The top of the core is placed horisontally in the upper left-hand corner. Each succeeding core section is laid below and parallel to the first, its top to the left. Viewing the core is the same as reading – left to right, top to bottom. <u>This system is recommended</u>.

17

2. Vertical book or Chinese:  In a box placed lengthwise away from the person, the top of core is placed in the upper left-hand corner.  Succeeding core segments are placed parallel to the previous segment, top of core at the top of the box.  Viewing the core is from the left to right, top to bottom.

Where possible the top and bottom of the core should be clearly shown on the core; they should always be shown by pencil or waterproof ink on the wood or cardboard on the inside of the box (not marked on the lid).  Any intervals of lost core or of core removed should be shown on a spacer; wooden plugs cut from 2 x 2 inch lumber work very well as spacers.  Failure to properly identify the top, bottom, and missing intervals can reduce the subsequent value of the core considerably, or render it useless.

When it is necessary to preserve the core moisture either rock or coal for subsequent analysis or other testing, the plastic should be sealed with tape.  Where it is necessary to maintain a near 100% humidity with the container, disposable diapers are very useful.  The diaper is moistened and placed in the core box, plastic side down, on top of the sealed plastic sheeting containing the core.

The cores should be packed firmly in the boxes to prevent shifting or rolling and other damage while transporting.  A good packing material in addition to the disposable diapers is fiberglass home-insulation material  in 16- or 23-inch wide rolls.  It is lightweight, is easily transported and stored, and can be cut to the desired widths and lengths. The core-box lid should be secured with a strong tape.  Nailing of wooden box lids should be avoided as jarring the boxes with a hammer may break the core.

Core sampling

General

Some of the information that may be derived from cores is
summarized below:

Geologic

Geochemical composition, including analyses for major oxides

and trace elements of overburden rock and coal, and proximate,

ultimate, Btu, and forms-of-sulfur analyses of coal (Swanson

and Huffman, 1976).

Stratigraphic determinations

Petrographic studies

Palynological examinations

Geophysical

Density

Seismic velocities

Resistivity and other electrical properties

Induced polarity

Engineering

Rock mechanics

Minability (surface and underground)

## Sampling

The well-site geologist has to decide the sample interval that will provide the maximum data consistent with the project's objectives.

Sampling of the non-coal parts of the core is usually done on a lithologic basis; that is, a sample is taken representing all core in sequence of similar lithology, regardless of length. For example, a core of mudstone 25 to 30 feet thick may contain a thin calcareous or siliceous zone and another zone of pyritic nodules; depending on the use to be made of the sample the mudstone could be one sample and the other zones separated as individual samples.

Coal sampling for overall coal bed quality is commonly done on a proportional basis, that is, each sample representing a given number of feet in proportion to the bed thickness. Where details of the coal bed quality is required, i.e., zones of high ash or sulphur, the sampling may be done, by changes in coal characteristics, rather than footage. Examples of this are taking separate roof and floor coal samples, hard and softer coal, etc. Ideally, where good quality geophysical logs are available, select the sample intervals based on these log data together with visual physical characteristics of the coal.

Sample bagging or sealing material should be a polyethylene or a similar plastic having a minimum thickness of 6 mils (0.006 inches). Bags of different sizes, as well as plastic sleeves or tubes of graduated diameters in rolls up to 1,000 feet, in length, are available. Plastic sheeting may also be used; however, it is harder to seal than tubes. The tubes are of special use when the core is packaged directly from the barrel without logging or washing. The sleeve can be slipped directly over the barrel and the core forced out as the barrel is withdrawn. The sleeve is also very handy for packaging short lengths of core to be used for various geophysical and engineering tests.

When bagging the samples sufficient water should be added to maintain as near as possible a 100% humidity within the container. This can be done by either dipping the core segments in clean water as they are bagged or adding small amount after bagging; normally the former is preferred. Any excess water in the bag, after filling and surface wetting of the coal, may be drained off.

After putting the core sample in the bag, the bag is pressed, forcing as much air out as is possible; the top should be twisted tight, folded over, and tightly secured with a strong tape. Plastic-coated wire ties can be used, but are not recommended where a tight seal is necessary to preserve moisture. Bare wire should not be used as it may cut through the bag.

Normally, single bagging is sufficient for non-coal samples; however, coal samples should be double bagged to assure moisture retention and to prevent the coal from cutting the bag which would result in drying and oxidation. Each bag should be sealed separately.

21

Two tags showing full identification of the core sample number, project name, hole number, footage represented, date, and name of geologist--should be made up. One tag is placed inside the one bag for rock samples and in the second bag for coal samples. It is a good idea to put the inside tag in a securely sealed small plastic bag, such as those available at local grocery stores. The second tag should be securely attached to the outside of the bag at the neck. While awaiting transportation, samples as well as cores should be stored in a dry location out of the direct sunlight.

# Selected references

Acker, W. L., III, 1974, Basic procedures for soil sampling and core core drilling:  Scranton, Pa., Acker Drill Co., Inc., 246 p.

Cumming, J. D., and Wickland, A. P., 1975, Diamond drill handbook: Toronto, Ontario, J. K. Smith & Sons, Diamond Products, Ltd., 547 p.

Division of Safety, Engineering and Research Center, 1973, Drillers safety manual: U.S. Bureau of Reclamation, 64 p.

Helms, C. A., 1976, Applications of electrical well logging techniques to identifying coal beds in the Powder River Basin, Wyoming: U.S. Geol. Survey Open-File Rept. 76-581, 58 p.

McCulloch, C. M., Levine, J. R., Kissell, F. N., Fuel, M., 1975, Measuring the methane content of bituminous coalbeds: U.S. Bur. Mines Rept. Inv. No. 8043, 22 p.

Schlumberger, 1972, Principles of Log interpretation, Volume 1: New York, Schlumberger, 113 p.

Schopf, J. M., 1960, Field description and sampling of coal beds: U.S. Geol. Survey Bull. 1111-B, p. 25-70.

Swanson, V. E., and Huffman, Claude, Jr., 1976, Guidelines for sample collecting and analytical methods used in the U.S. Geological Survey for determining chemical composition of coal:  U.S. Geol. Survey Circ. 735, 11 p.

CPSIA information can be obtained at www.ICGtesting.com
Printed in the USA
BVOW05s1218190813

328997BV00002B/9/P